TINY MOO[

'Funny, compact and beauti[   ]
Simon Winder, *New Statesman*

'This small-press gem is perfect for
devouring in one sitting.' Emily Polson, *Book Riot*

'Throughout *Tiny Moons* the past mingles with the
present, tempting the reader with the aromas, tastes
and textures of the many dishes and snacks that
Powles writes about so exquisitely and tenderly.'
Chris Tse, *Pantograph Punch*

'Enjoy *Tiny Moons* for Powles' tales of eating sticky,
savoury buns and sizzling ginger & garlicky pork
dumplings; for the sense of escape to an unknown
city while we're so rooted at home; or for the lyrical
beauty of her prose.' Julie Vuong, *oh mag*

'Intelligent, poetic and entertaining, *Tiny Moons* is
at once an intimate, personal account of Chinese
food that will make you crave dumplings and
noodles, as well as a profound contemplation on the
notions of cultural hybridity, emotional landscapes
and belonging.' Jennifer Wong, *Cha Journal*

TINY MOONS

A YEAR OF EATING
IN SHANGHAI

Nina Mingya Powles

ILLUSTRATED BY
EMMA DAI'AN WRIGHT

THE EMMA PRESS

First published in the UK in 2020 by the Emma Press Ltd.

Reprinted in 2021 and 2022.

Text © Nina Mingya Powles 2020.
Illustrations © Emma Dai'an Wright 2020.

Edited by Emma Dai'an Wright and Yen-Yen Lu.
Glossary by David Wright.

ISBN 978-1-912915-34-7

A CIP catalogue record of this book
is available from the British Library.

Printed and bound in Latvia by Jelgavas Tipogrāfija.

The Emma Press
theemmapress.com
hello@theemmapress.com
Birmingham, UK

LOTTERY FUNDED · Supported using public funding by ARTS COUNCIL ENGLAND

CONTENTS

Hungry Girls 1

WINTER

锅贴 / Pan-fried Dumplings 8
葱油拌面/ Spring Onion Oil Noodles 14

SPRING

菠萝包 / Pineapple Buns 19
pisang goreng / Banana Fritters 27

SUMMER

芝麻饼 / Sesame Pancakes 34
粽子 / Sticky Rice Dumplings 39
馄饨面 / Wonton Noodle Soup 49

AUTUMN

上海早饭 / Breakfast in Shanghai 55
茄子 / Chinese Aubergines 63

WINTER AGAIN

饺子 / Boiled Dumplings 75

Acknowledgements *86*
About the author *87*
About the illustrator *87*
About The Emma Press *87*
Glossary *88*

Hungry Girls

A pair of pink plastic chopsticks. A bowl full of instant noodles. The smell of chicken stock and jasmine tea. Steam starts to tickle my nose. Popo, my grandmother, watches me from her lacquered chair.

This is one of my very early memories, where the shapes are blurred and colours flare out in waves. Pink and yellow plastic, deep blue Tibetan carpet. I don't know if all the parts are real, but I do know what happened next. When no one was looking, I flipped the bowl. The rim hit the table with a clatter, flinging out noodles and sending my chopsticks onto the floor. My mother shouted *Aiyah!* as I knew she would. But in the memory-dream, Popo doesn't move. She sits still, watching me.

I only wanted to make a mess, but I think this might have been my first act of rebellion. No more chopsticks. No more noodles, at least not today.

This was short-lived, of course. I ate noodles willingly nearly every day growing up, so much so that they were known as Nina Noodles at my aunt and uncle's house.

But there came a time, when I was about five, when I started to hate my weekend Chinese classes. I had bad dreams about the red and gold banners strung across the doorways and the high-pitched songs they made us sing. None of the other kids looked like me. None of their dads looked like mine. The languages and dialects they spoke with their parents sounded familiar to me, and I recognised a few words, but I wasn't able to join in. I stopped attending the classes. Eventually my mother stopped using Chinese at home, or maybe I just stopped listening. Words vanished, along with the sounds.

ming 明 / *a sun* 日 *next to a moon* 月
ya 雅 / *a tooth* 牙 *next to a bird* 隹

◄◄◄

Big hips, brown eyes, and brown hair that turns lighter during a Aotearoa New Zealand summer. The way I look means that people can't usually tell that I'm half Malaysian-Chinese. The way I look has given me enormous privilege my whole life, in a series of predominantly pakeha[1] spaces: a white school, white university (in the English and Creative Writing departments at least), white suburb, white poetry readings. It means I can lie when a guy approaches me in a bar to say he really likes mixed girls and asks, 'Can I guess your ethnicity?' It makes it easy for some white people to see me as the same as them.

My grandfather, Gung Gung, picked my Chinese name when I was born. It's also my middle name: 明雅, Mingya, meaning something like 'bright elegance'. I only really learned to say it correctly when I was

---

1 New Zealanders of European descent

seventeen (*rising tone, falling-rising tone*) and only learned how to write the characters when I was twenty, after years of ducking out of the classroom game of what's-your-middle-name, muttering 'Never mind, it's Chinese', as if that were the same as not having one at all.

◀◀

I starved myself of language, but I couldn't starve myself of other things. Wonton noodle soup, Cantonese roast duck, my mother's crispy egg noodles and her special congee. All the thick, sweet smells of yum cha restaurants my parents took me to, ordering all the same dishes every time, ever since I was born. I remember peeling pieces of rice paper from steaming charsiu bao and scrunching them into paper flowers. I remember drawing one of the few Chinese characters I knew on the steamed-up glass with my finger: 米, mi, the character for rice, like an open flower or a six-point star.

We moved to Shanghai when I was twelve, and I encountered a whole new landscape of sound: voices chattering in rising-falling waves, chaotic but familiar. I built myself a new home with new colours, new friends, and new foods: mooncakes, sesame pancakes, fried aubergine, black tea, and dumplings.

◄◄◄

To remember, to *re-member*. Remembering as the opposite of dismembering. To put something back together again. A sun next to a moon, a tooth next to a bird.

I taught myself to cook around the same time I decided to take Chinese as one of my subject majors at university back in Wellington, along with English Literature. I was hungry to create, to make things with my hands, to relearn and recover what I'd lost.

Xu Ayi, our family's housekeeper in Shanghai, had written down her recipe for jiaozi, dumplings, and given it to my mother. My mother translated it into English and copied it carefully into her cut-and-paste recipe book made of scraps of newspaper and magazines. I used this recipe in my Kelburn student flat, trying out different fillings depending on which vegetables were cheapest at the market: spinach instead of Chinese cabbage, spring onions instead of chives. I researched all the different ways of making cong youbing, spring onion pancakes, and combined them into my own method, kneading and folding the dough early in the morning before class so it would be ready to fry that night.

When she was younger, Popo was a brilliant cook. The kitchen was hers and hers alone. She always had something cooking, some soup or congee made from the bones of last night's meat. I can't speak Hakka, the Chinese dialect my mother's family speak at home, so I only had simple conversations with her, in a mix of Mandarin and English, before her health deteriorated and speech wasn't really possible anymore. I wish I had thought to ask: what's your favourite dish to cook? Which flavours remind you of when you were little? What did your mother teach you?

On a visit to Malaysia a few years ago, the last time Popo was healthy and lucid enough to talk with us, my mother acting as translator as usual, I asked for the recipe of her chicken and aubergine curry. It was years since she last cooked but still she knew it by heart. After dinner, the three of us sat round the table: Popo explaining the steps in Hakka, Mum translating into English, me writing everything down. In the background I could hear Gung Gung watching a Cantonese soap opera upstairs and the soft clicking of moths and mosquitoes flying at the netted windows.

When I last saw her, six months before she passed away, Popo could never remember whether she'd turned the light off in the upstairs rooms, going back to check again and again. She couldn't remember if she'd offered you a napkin, so she'd offer you another and another. But some things are harder to forget.

‹‹‹

女 *(woman, feminine): I see a curved standstill /*
a breath being held in /

It is tiring to be a woman who loves to eat in a society where hunger is something not to be satisfied but controlled. Where a long history of female hunger is associated with shame and madness. The body must be punished for every misstep; for every "indulgence" the balance of control must be restored. To enjoy food as a young woman, to opt out every day from the guilt expected of me, is a radical act, of love. My body often feels like it's neither here nor there. Too much like this, not enough like that. But however it looks, my body allows me to feel hunger.

We must have been fourteen or fifteen, eating burgers at our favourite expat American diner in Shanghai, licking salt and ketchup off our fingers. We were best friends: two half-Chinese girls, one with hair darker than the other, one a little taller, both with our nails painted black. An older white man came up close to our table. 'You two must be hungry girls,' he said, raising an eyebrow and walking on. We stared after him, mouthed *What the fuck.* Then we looked at each other and started

6

to laugh because we didn't know what he meant exactly, only that it was true.

◄◄◄

I've been learning Mandarin for over three years now but there are still days when language fails me, when food feels like the only thing I have to tie me to this other home my family brought to me from far away.

There are things that pass from one hand to another, from mothers to daughters, from sister to sister, between cousins, between friends. A hot curry puff fresh from the oven, a secret batter recipe, a special technique for slicing mango.

One day I tried making Popo's curry in my flat in Wellington. I read all the ingredient labels of all the curry powders in the supermarket to find the closest match: coriander seeds, cumin, fennel, chilli, turmeric, cinnamon, cloves, pepper, cardamom. The richly-scented list repeated like an incantation in my head. I bought fresh roti canai from Kelburn Parade and carried it home through a southerly storm. The curry turned out badly: watery, flavourless, the aubergine overcooked. But for a while my little kitchen smelled like cumin and coconut and crushed ginger. Like running in from the tropical rain, like Popo ladling rice into our bowls, like the lit mosquito coil and the flame lighting up my mother's hands as she carries it towards me. These things I don't need language to understand.

WINTER

season of baby mandarins, apples

Pan-fried Dumplings
锅贴

On a Saturday morning I wait in line at my local Yang's Dumplings, just down the road from my university in Shanghai. The air smells of hot oil and toasted sesame seeds. I watch clouds of steam collect near the ceiling. As the lunch rush approaches, noise builds in the food court.

The regulars and the serving staff are used to me by now. Only a few older aunties stare at me, and when I smile back at them they look away, amused. A little boy waiting in line behind me bumps my hip and his father apologises in English, embarrassed. 'Mei guanxi,' I reply – *no worries*. He looks surprised for half a second, then turns back to his phone. 'Wo e *si*le,' the boy moans repeatedly. *I'm so hungry I'm gonna die.* Me too.

There are no chairs, only one long stainless steel bench where grandmas and grandkids sit elbow-to-elbow, shovelling soup and dumplings drenched in chilli oil into their mouths. I can't read the whole menu but it doesn't matter, because the way it works here is there are two windows where you queue for two kinds of dumplings: the famous shengjianbao (fried soup dumplings) and guotie (pan-fried dumplings). I hand the chef my order receipt and he piles four fat guotie into a plastic container. He points me to the vinegar-and-chopsticks station even though I swear he must recognise me – how could he not? I come in almost every day. But he offers no sign of recognition, and returns grumpily to doling out more dumplings.

I eat my guotie right there, standing beneath the fluorescent lights. First the crunch, then hot soup scalds my tongue – I wasn't expecting so much soup – then gingery, garlicky pork in the middle. I've got soup in my hair and all over my chin and there's an auntie staring at me who finds this very funny, but I don't care. I take a bite and my worries melt away. I'm home and also far away from home, in one bite.

◀◀

I arrived in Shanghai near the end of winter, in February, to take up the Chinese government scholarship that allowed me to study Mandarin full-time for one year, with a small room of my own on the university campus. The day I arrived I felt dazed, blinking through the thick winter smog. My first meal at the campus cafeteria consisted of cold pickled vegetables, wilting stir-fried cauliflower with slivers of beancurd skin and plain steamed rice. Chinese cauliflower is picked late in the season so the florets are smaller, with tougher stalks, chewy but not unpleasant. I hadn't yet learned that Chinese students eat lunch as early as eleven o'clock; by early afternoon, the lunch hour is long finished and there's hardly any food left. I was hungry enough for anything, but as I ate my way through this cold meal I felt homesick. I hadn't expected to feel so lonely so soon. Back in my dorm room, I unpacked my warmest winter clothes. The room was about one metre wide and two metres long, with a bed, a desk and a small wardrobe, and a tiled floor and piece of foam for a mattress. No kitchen, and it was tiny, but it was mine.

In my first week as a liuxuesheng (foreign student), I tried all kinds of dumplings I had never seen before. Shanghai-style shaomai with sticky rice and shiitake mushrooms on top; the famous soup-filled xiaolongbao, to dip carefully in a mix of vinegar and soy sauce and top with thin strips of fresh ginger before taking a bite. But after six days of new dumpling adventures, I craved something more familiar.

Guotie (the name literally translates to 'stuck to the pot') are the pan-fried version of shuijiao, boiled dumplings. They are half steamed and half fried, to make their bottoms crisp and their skins tender.

There is nothing like the sound of water hissing as it hits the wok and the lid being clamped down over it.

When I was a teenager in Shanghai, Xu Ayi made guotie in our kitchen almost every day. I came home from school to the sharp smell of vinegar and the sound of her smashing cloves of garlic on the kitchen counter. I watched her mix Shaoxing cooking wine with soy sauce and a cold beaten egg, then add minced pork, chives, garlic, ginger and white pepper to the blue-rimmed enamel bowl. She didn't make her own dough for the skin, but bought bags of fresh wrappers from the market around the corner.

She showed us how to pleat and fold the dumplings, but my mother and I were never very good. My mother grew up eating mostly Cantonese, Hakka and Malay Chinese food and so didn't learn how to fold these types of wheat dumplings, which originate from northern China. Xu Ayi took the round wrapper in her palm, dabbed a little water around the edge for glue, and spooned a bit of the pork into the middle. Her expert fingers sealed each one shut with four folds, spaced evenly along one side of the curve. On a plastic tray printed with a border of blue roses, she laid them out like rows of small crescent moons.

We took this recipe back home with us too, and tried to recreate it. Our efforts were good enough: we made them almost every week when I was sixteen or seventeen, filling and folding them on trays balanced in our laps as we watched our favourite cooking shows – Rick Stein or Anthony Bourdain – on TV. But the xianr, the filling, was never quite the same. The difference was subtle: not the ingredients or seasonings, but the texture, the ratio of soft-to-crunch, the weight and feel of holding one in the air between two chopsticks. Maybe it's impossible to recreate the exact weight of a memory, but we keep trying.

◀◀

The harsh cold has retreated a little in Shanghai. It feels like something has softened inside the air, a bit of blue returning to the sky, and it's lighter in the evening. I've recovered from the flu enough to get up and put on my normal clothes. After days spent in bed, the moment I'm out and about I'm viciously hungry. I head down the road to my nearest dumpling joint, the name of which I can't yet decipher. I try to sound out the familiar parts of each unfamiliar character. The staff wear orange t-shirts and the girl at the counter has stick-on jewels on her nails. At seven in the evening, long after most families have gone home, students seem to be sitting in groups at the tables but when I look closer I see they are actually eating alone, watching TV shows and music videos on their iPhones propped up against the chopstick dispensers. No one looks up when I sit down.

The guotie are cheap here, five yuan for a plate of four. In what I'm beginning to learn must be the typical Shanghai style, the dumpling skin is almost as thick as the dough used for shengjianbao, pan-fried buns, which makes for extra crunchy bottoms. They come sprinkled with black sesame seeds and chopped spring onions. These Shanghai guotie aren't like Xu Ayi's: they are big and hearty, filled with soup as well as meat.

They taste like eating breakfast with my mother with the radio on in the background, or having dinner in my Kelburn flat with the windows steamed up. They taste like that one winter when I went on a language exchange programme in Beijing in my second year of university, when I thought I might die from cold and homesickness and dumplings were the only cure. But they are also new and unfamiliar.

Walking home after dinner, I pause before crossing the road and watch steam rise above the man tossing strips of meat in hot chilli oil and sesame paste at his food cart. I get distracted by the sky. It's well after dark, but the sky is light purple, burnt orange around the edges. I've started to notice what the smog does to the sky round here, the way it warps light and colours. Forgetting for a moment that green walking signals are meaningless, I almost walk into a bus. A rookie mistake, but I'm learning. A girl asks me for directions in Mandarin and I find I can give them to her – in Mandarin. I am learning to cross the road like I know where I'm going. I am learning to stab the dumpling with one chopstick to let the hot soup cool before I take a bite.

Spring Onion Oil Noodles

葱油拌面

One weekend we sit huddled together on a bench in a narrow lane, eating noodles out of cardboard containers balanced on our knees. It begins to rain. It's March, the harsh edge of winter still present in the air at night, but this has the taste of summer rain: warm, fragrant, heavy. I'm with two of my classmates and we are deep inside a maze of picturesque lanes known as Tianzifang. The place is packed full of tourists, us included. We sit on one side of a sea of umbrellas and selfie sticks, blinking steam and rain from our eyes.

Where tourists abound in Shanghai, so does overpriced Western food. We could have picked anything: waffles, sandwiches, New York-style pizza, Chicago-style pizza, spaghetti bolognese. We've taken one bus and three subway lines to get here. But when you are tired and hungry and it's starting to rain, there is only one thing that will do.

◀◀◀

When I learned that congyou banmian (literally 'spring onion oil mixed noodles') existed, I had a feeling they might become a big part of my life. The dish consists of a bowl of fine hand-pulled noodles tossed with spring onion-infused oil, dark soy sauce (the thicker, sweeter kind), and strips of spring onions that have been fried slowly in a lot of oil until dark and bittersweet, crisp and caramelised.

This is Shanghai's answer to cacio e pepe: simple, satisfying. And as with most Italian pasta dishes, the magic lies in the noodles-to-sauce ratio. Here, the ratio usually sits at an excellent 7:3. A modest amount of sauce, and an unspeakably huge amount of noodles.

The chef spoons the oil and the crispy onions over a thick wad of noodles. The smell reaches the table before the bowl does – rich, warm and bitter, a little sweetness in the tang of soy sauce. I use my chopsticks to mix it all together myself. Then I demolish it. With some practice, I learn not to regret it. I begin to think of those fried spring onions as a genuine part of my daily vegetable intake. I begin to prioritise joy.

◀◀

Congyou banmian are often called 'banmian' for short. At breakfast and lunch (and dinner, if you're like me) people shout this across counters and tabletops all over Shanghai. The sharp falling tone of each word makes me want to say them louder, give them

more oomph, like a swear word. Sometimes the cashier knows what's up before the second syllable has left my mouth. She nods at me, serious and businesslike.

It's become a kind of ritual. I ride my bike to the food mall at Wujiaochang after class, I order my noodles, I collect my chopsticks from the little chopstick washer and dispenser that hums pleasantly in the corner, and I sit at the bench full of people dining alone, more than half of them eating banmian.

Back in Wellington, I do things alone all the time during the day. I work, I eat, I write, I go for walks. But at night, things change. At night, aloneness in a public space means strange looks and unwanted attention. It means knowing the quickest, safest route home, pretending to talk on the phone and gripping my keys inside my pocket. But here, perhaps like in all big cities, aloneness is part of the city itself. In Shanghai I almost never feel un-safe. I walk long distances with my earphones in, never once needing to cross the road to avoid groups of loud, obnoxious men. I ride my bike through the campus without once glancing behind me. It's partly my white-passing privilege that affords me this feeling of freedom and safety, but I see many local students around me doing the same. I order my noodles and eat them in peace and, for a little while, I feel less like an outsider.

◄◄◄

Winter is nearly over and the downpours have begun. This is the beginning of the Plum Rains, Shanghai's infamous rainy season, named after the time when plums traditionally begin to ripen. *Plum rains.* I can taste the rain, sweet and full. At this time of year the sky is dark violet and gold at dusk. The Chinese for Plum Rains is 梅雨, meiyu. The end of the second syllable melts in my mouth. In the early afternoon, during the third downpour of the day, I step out of my dorm building and wonder if I will make it to class. I have never seen so much water fall from the sky. I have never heard rain make so much noise. It streams down the sides of my umbrella and sloshes me in the face. Bikes and scooters tear through the water all around me, small waves breaking against the footpath. I set off into the underwater city, my boots instantly filling up. Just as I'm arriving, the rain suddenly stops and everything is still. The effect is dizzying: all the leaves shaking, umbrellas opening and closing. The air smells like mud and crushed flowers.

It rains a fourth time when I head to the nearest dumpling-and-noodle joint for dinner. It's not my favourite but it's the cheapest, which counts for a lot when you live in Shanghai on a student budget. The road is splashed across with pink and green from the neon lights above. Steam, or steamy smog, seems to be rising up.

Another benefit to eating alone is that the only person you can splatter with soy sauce is yourself. Like all the best foods, banmian are messy. They are impossible to eat with any degree of restraint or elegance. With each bite I feel increasingly powerful and glorious, like some kind of fierce mythical creature who feasts only on soy sauce noodles. In the corner of my eye I see the man next to me devouring his banmian alongside a plate of six fluffy, crispy, soupy shengjianbao. This is a level of Shanghai hardcore I have not yet reached, but I'll get there.

◀◀◀

Each time I'm at a new eatery where the menu is only in Chinese, I take a picture of it on my phone and look up the words I don't know later. This is how I discover new ways to eat.

葱

The character 葱, cong, meaning 'spring onion', is one of my favourites. Complex and elegant, it is made up of twelve short strokes that fit closely together like a cluster of leaves. Or like the shreds of crisp onions left at the bottom of the bowl. When 葱 is combined with 绿, lü (meaning 'green'), it becomes 'lush green'. Bright green, verdant. A colour you don't see so much here in the middle of the city, except in food: handfuls sprinkled over dumplings, into bowls of noodles, over pieces of dough being kneaded and rolled out by the old man in the white cap. I can taste it.

SPRING

season of soft strawberries,
grapes, nashi pears, papaya

Pineapple Buns
菠萝包

Lately the weather in Shanghai has been reminding me of when I was fourteen and attending an international high school on the edge of the city, when we used to sit on the grass after school drinking mango smoothies and watching boys with bad haircuts skateboard across the hot concrete. It always smelled of sweat and damp grass. As May drew closer the rain became heavier and fell in frequent, violent bursts. It was getting hot, but nothing like the bright shockwave of heat that always came in June. The taste of summer was just within reach and we were restless.

My earliest childhood impressions are ones where I am just about to eat something. The smell of something delicious floods the entire room of my memory, beckoning me closer: two-minute noodles and plastic chopsticks, apple juice in green cups, chocolate ice cream covered in sprinkles, buttered toast with the crusts cut off, the thin rice paper on the bottoms of warm, fluffy charsiu bao.

19

I am sitting beneath a cherry blossom tree in a grassy area of campus, doing my Mandarin homework, when the teenage-dream pre-summer smell hits me. Soaked grass, warm skin, and something artificially sweet like raspberry lip balm. It must be because of the heady dusk sky slowly turning the colour of peach iced tea, and the warmth, the terrible humidity that makes my hair frizzier each day. Living in Shanghai again, this time as an adult, the taste-memories come rushing back: crispy dumplings, spring onion and sesame pancakes, Starbucks blueberry muffins (which still taste just the same), cinnamon-coated pretzels, waffle fries from the cafeteria, mango ice cream, and warm boluo bao – pineapple buns.

◀◀

I can't remember my first boluo bao in any great detail, but they are in the background of almost all my childhood memories: shining lusciously from Chinese bakery windows whenever we went to visit family in Singapore, Malaysia or Hong Kong; being whirled around on vast trays carried by waiters at Cantonese restaurants. Their butter-sweet aroma and bright yellow tops light up the streets of many Asian cities and Chinatowns, welcoming me home.

Like most of the things I love to eat, boluo bao are not fancy. They are about the size of a bagel and made of fluffy, sweet dough with a crumbly, sugary, bright yellow coating on top. That's it. The name literally means 'pineapple bread', but the bun contains no trace of actual pineapples as far as I can tell. The only link, as my Aunty Bin pointed out to me once in a comment on my Instagram post, is that when  the yellow topping is decorated in a criss-cross pattern it vaguely resembles a pineapple. But the name is perfect nonetheless, full of sunshine yellow.

The origins of boluo bao are unknown, but since the 1900s they have been an afternoon tea staple in Hong Kong's beloved cha chaan tengs. Cha chaan teng means 'tea restaurant' in Cantonese (cha canting in Mandarin) but these places are much more than that. There is one in Shanghai, hidden on a quiet street that splits off from chaotic Huahai Zhong Lu. The neon sign hanging in the window, "茶餐厅", spills pink and green light onto the wet pavement. There is always a queue, and you will always have to share a small table with people you don't know. The walls are a pale greenish-brown, with retro screens of yellow and blue glass tiles separating smokers from the non-smokers. It's like stepping into *Chungking Express*, Wong Kar Wai's film set in 1990s Hong Kong, with its cool palette of jade green and soft aquamarine. When I first saw the film I recognised the colours instantly, and the way the characters always seemed to be looking at each other through a haze of steam and city smog. At the back of the restaurant, where plates of food arrive clattering from the kitchen onto steel counters, the shelves are stacked with tins of condensed milk, Bovril, soup and packets of instant noodles. The menu is what you might call 'Canto-Western' or, as it's known colloquially, 'soy sauce Western food'. When Hong Kong was a British colony, cha chaan tengs emerged as a cheap option for those wanting Western food, which was usually only available at high-end restaurants. As a result, here are all the wondrous comfort foods of my childhood somehow listed on a single menu: fried noodles and fried rice, soy sauce chicken and roast goose, pork buns and fried wontons, along with spaghetti, macaroni, tinned soup, corned beef, sandwiches and toast of all kinds. Peanut butter toast, sugar toast, condensed milk toast, and Hong Kong-style deep-fried French toast.

The most exquisite item on the menu, in my opinion, is the boluo bao. It arrives at my table moments after the waitress takes my order. It's warm and glistening, with a centimetre-thick slab of soft butter sandwiched inside, melting into the bun. The runner-up is the banana split, which in Mandarin is called xiangjiaochuan, a banana *boat*. It's an intricate, perfect creation: one scoop each of strawberry, chocolate and vanilla ice cream atop two halves of banana, topped with drizzled chocolate syrup, a whorl of whipped cream from a can, and rainbow sprinkles. When it arrives, we are wide-eyed with wonder. Three friends hover spoons over the ice cream, unwilling to be the first to take a bite and ruin this masterpiece. The couple sharing our table eye our dessert approvingly. They take sips of cold milk tea while finishing off the last of their deep-fried shrimp toast. Hong Kong natives, Cantonese food lovers and fellow homesick students congregate here at this place that feels caught in time. My upbringing between two cultures converges in this smoky, tea-and-butter scented cha chaan teng, open late every night.

◀◀

For a long time I didn't know what boluo bao were called in English. My introduction to Mandarin, Cantonese and Hakka, the three languages my mother and her family all speak, was through food. The first Mandarin words my mother taught me when I was little were niunai (milk) and mianbao (bread). She says this is because, as a child, I was always happiest when eating and unhappiest when hungry. Along with boluo bao, I grew up with Cantonese dim sum staples such as har gow (steamed shrimp dumplings), siu mai (shrimp and pork dumplings), charsiu bao (barbecue pork buns), and luobogao (fried turnip cake). It was only when I got older and occasionally had yum cha with friends that I realised I didn't know the English names. To me, English words don't quite exist for these dishes. 'Steamed shrimp dumpling' could mean any shrimp dumpling, not the delicately folded spheres of translucent skin that are har gow. Until we moved to China, these were the only scraps of Cantonese and Mandarin that I knew. But I knew them well. It's with words like these that I was able to talk with Popo. 'Ni chile ma? Chi baole ma?' *Have you eaten? Are you full?*

◄◄

I pass several bakeries on my usual route between the university and subway station. I often end up biking home with a paper bag in my basket, a warm boluo bao inside. Whatever the time of year, they remind me of sun, tropical heat, being with family. Mooncakes, the little cakes eaten during the Mid-Autumn Festival, are meant to look like moons. Boluo bao look like shining suns.

The sun is out when I stop by Tsui Wah Restaurant & Bakery. I'd never noticed this place before until one day, on my way home, I spotted a man coming out of the kitchen carrying an enormous tray of shining buns, straight from the oven, steam still coming off them as he slid them one by one into the bakery cabinet.

Shanghainese people know how to snack. Here, entire floors of giant supermarkets are dedicated to snack-food: crackers, nuts, cakes, cookies, candy, dried fruits, dried meat, dried fish, dried octopus, dried everything.

The Chinese bakeries play a fundamental role in snack-food culture too. At all hours of the day they are crammed with grandmas and grandpas piling trays full of pastries, buns, and loaves of bread. The warm smells waft out into the street. Sugar, yeast, melted butter. Standing in the boluo bao queue at Tsui Wah Restaurant & Bakery I can see right into the kitchen, where two bakers wearing white hats roll pieces of dough into fat balls. For the crumbly topping, the most important part, they cut large sheets of golden icing into squares and lay one over each bun. They brush them generously with egg for extra shine. If you don't get your boluo bao to go, it arrives cut in half and with a slice of butter in the middle. Butter or no butter, a boluo bao is beautiful and satisfying, best enjoyed while biking home in late spring.

◀◀

Homesickness comes in waves, sometimes leaving me reeling. It can hit at any moment, but most often when I'm in my dorm room alone. I scroll through news from home, especially on GeoNet, which maps seismic activity in real-time across the whole of Aotearoa. When fissures erupt and small earthquakes and their aftershocks hit home, I feel them in my dreams. I long to be back by the sea, surrounded by shades of green and wildflowers turning gold on the hills.

At the campus fruit shop where a lady sits outside carving pineapples, I spend some time taking in all the colours.

Later, I write them down in my notebook and fill myself up on them. Hot pink dragon fruit, glowing mangoes, fluorescent oranges, watermelons, blush-orange papaya, strawberries so red and soft they might burst. I notice the gutters full of crushed plum blossom from last night's rain. At night I notice the sky: dark, molten purple. I notice the lights at night, the way they disperse weirdly in the fog, blue and green clouds eating each other above the buildings. I notice how sunlight falls in diagonal lines across my small balcony for a few hours each day. After a while, it warms.

Banana Fritters

pisang goreng

At school in Wellington we learned how to do a mihi, a traditional way of introducing yourself in Māori where you give the name of your maunga (mountain), your awa (river), your moana (sea) and your iwi (people), and – finally – your name. It's about indicating your closeness to the land, the water and the people who make you who you are.

I never used to feel linked to any particular mountain or sea or river, never saw them as a part of myself. I have left several homes and created new ones. Home has always been complicated. But there is a mountain I do keep coming back to: Mount Kinabalu in Kota Kinabalu, Malaysia, a small city on the northeast coast of the island of Borneo, where my mother was born and raised. This is my mountain, though I've never lived anywhere near it.

◄◄◄

At the end of May, during mid-term break, I fly to Kota Kinabalu to meet my parents. Popo and Gung Gung still live in the same old house with the yellow flame tree above the front door, and coconut palms and a mango tree in the backyard. Usually these visits mean long, hot days spent lounging under the ceiling fans, reading my mother's old Agatha Christie collection and watching

Cantonese soap operas. But now there are cousins and uncles arriving each day from Singapore and Kuala Lumpur. The big old house, usually empty, is full of voices shouting across each other in various combinations of Hakka and English and Chinese and Malay. There are ten pairs of flip-flops piled up by the front door. The house has high ceilings and hard floors and windows covered in mosquito nets. The house is always full of echoes. Warm air carries sound just the same way it always has since I was little: slow, heavy, drifting through the walls. It's like the air is so thick and warm that sounds get trapped inside it, like insects caught in the folds of mosquito nets hung from the ceiling. Even the faintest noises echo throughout the house. Dragonflies hitting the windows, green geckos chirping from the window sills, Gung Gung's slippers shuffling along the tiles, the whirr of electric ceiling fans, the clock in the hall that chimes every half hour. The geckos grow louder at night. We call them chit-chuks, using our teeth to imitate their sound.

The house is the same every time I come back. As soon as I step inside, the familiar smells hit me: burning mosquito coils, old books, and a mix of ginger, cloves and curry paste wafting in from the kitchen.

My mother's family all speak Hakka, a southern Chinese dialect spoken in China itself and in many diasporic Chinese communities around the world, including in

Malaysia. I grew up with the sound of Hakka around me, though I can't speak it. Since I do speak some Mandarin, sometimes I feel more connected to my Asian heritage through mainland Chinese culture and language, rather than through Malaysia. Sometimes I feel like I have no right to claim any part of my Asian-ness, given that I mostly look and sound white. Living and travelling through Asia as a half-Asian woman means moving between different versions of myself: Western tourist, foreign student, writer, language learner, a person trying to understand more about her heritage. I now know there are many different ways of travelling through the world. Some of us are more prone than others to leaving bits of ourselves behind.

◀◀

There are some parts of Kota Kinabalu that I carry with me always. The mountain, so often hidden by rainforest clouds, only appearing momentarily over the city in the early morning. The way the rain comes down in the late afternoon, violently and without warning. Iridescent blue dragonflies, white egrets and giant moths with patterned wings. And food – the thing that anchors me here. Open-air restaurants where we sit on stools and eat bowls of fresh Hokkien noodles with orange plastic chopsticks, sipping teh tarek – iced milk tea so sweet it makes your teeth ache – and the air full of coconut-milk steam, my eyes watering from chilli sauce and the afternoon heat.

This May, sometime between four and five one morning, the pre-dawn light sifts through the curtains and leaves a pattern of leaves on the bedroom ceiling. I sleep in the same room always, the one that was my uncle's when he was a child. The distant song of the mosque's morning call-to-prayer drifts in. The wavering voice is crystal clear, interspersed with quiet birdsong. I can't understand any of the words but there are moments I can feel the singer mourning something. I can feel the song's low notes reverberating in the bottom of my ribcage. I hear Gung Gung getting up, shuffling down the corridor, switching on the news. Gradually more noises float up the stairs, and more smells: toast, coffee, reheated fried noodles.

We all wake early in the heat, but I'm still the last to the breakfast table. Gung Gung is much older now and doesn't go to the market so often, but he and my uncle have made a special trip for our visit. They always return with the same pink bags, handles knotted together at the top. On the table there are wodges of creamy durian, which my mother loves but no one else can bear. Fresh red papaya cut into cubes, yellow mangoes, stringy jackfruit, lychees, prickly-skinned rambutan, bunches of tiny bananas. There are colourful glutinous rice cakes, some with bean or peanut paste inside. Wobbly cubes in rainbow layers of cotton-candy pink, jade green and blushing red, and soft coconut-white balls that leave a ring of powdered sugar on my lips when I bite into them.

Then there are the pisang goreng – banana fritters. Gung Gung brings home extra when Mum and I are visiting. He tips the golden fried bananas onto a blue enamel platter, covering them with a tray to keep them warm and keep the flies away. The room fills with the scent of hot oil, sesame, sugar, coconut.

A freshly-fried banana is crunchy when you bite into it. The batter is almost savoury, contrasting with the caramel taste of these particular tropical bananas, known as ladyfinger or sugar bananas. They are so sweet that my tongue tingles if I eat too many. When I take my first bite after years away from Kota Kinabalu, I taste tropical heat. I can taste the slow hours spent in the back garden beneath the mango tree, spotting lizards in the tall grass. I taste the fierce sun on my neck, only ever bearable on days when we went swimming at the Sabah Golf Club and ate choco- late ice cream afterwards in the shade.

I dream of the smell of fresh pisang goreng in the morning, crisp and golden and sweet.

They're almost better in the afternoon, softened but not soggy, when the crust has changed from crisp to chewy. When we leave Kota Kinabalu, Mum and I always wrap a handful of cold banana fritters in paper napkins and pack them in our hand luggage. We eat them with our fingers while watching planes take off into the shimmering heat at the end of the runway.

‹‹‹

We snack on pisang goreng while driving up the winding road towards big, blue Mount Kinabalu. The rocky summit disappears and reappears from behind dark rainclouds. Every time it appears, I can see more and more waterfalls streaming down the steep rainforest cliffs, some of them starting far above the cloudline. I follow the white line of water down as far as I can see.

We visited Kinabalu National Park when I was little, but all I remember is fog, humidity, and vines hanging over the road like scenes from *The Jungle Book*. I also remember blue butterflies, real live ones with wings that turned violet when they caught the light, their wingspan bigger than my two hands put together. But I don't know if I just imagined these, especially as blue butterflies are rare and endangered, only to be found enclosed in butterfly houses or framed and pinned to the wall at the Sabah Museum. When I was six, I was obsessed with the idea of catching a glimpse of them in the wild, poring over glossy pictures in the ancient, falling-apart copies of *National Geographic* that Gung Gung has collected since the 1950s and never thrown out. Like many of my childhood obsessions, they became real to me.

As we drive back down the mountain road we are sleepy from the heat, and so full from all the bananas. A tropical thunderstorm has started, so loud we can't hear ourselves speak, so we don't. It's warm and my skin is damp. I think I smell like the rainforest. Maybe my body of water is the rainforest or the whole city in the rain; maybe my rivers are all these small waterfalls. I can't see anything outside through the mist except occasional flashes of banana tree fields. I keep looking back until they disappear.

SUMMER

season of pineapples, black plums,
white peaches, an abundance of watermelon

Sesame Pancakes

芝麻饼

We go on days when the sun is out, when the air is full of seed pods floating down from the plane trees, getting in our eyes and in our hair. We go when it is pouring down with rain, a violent kind of rain, with heavy drops that make a sound as they hit the skin. We go despite the humidity that is gradually becoming unbearable, even in May.

The place is Zhengsu Lu, a little snack street five minutes from where my classes are held. There's a man selling baozi on the corner, his vegetable buns a warm hug, and across the road there's a wonton place with a sesame chilli dipping sauce that is legendary among students. On another corner there's the fruit shop where the lady likes to chat to me about my family as she chops the heads off pineapples with a cleaver.

There's a lamian noodle shop too, where I like to watch the boss's son, the noodle-making apprentice, standing in a cloud of flour while stretching and spinning long pieces of dough. He throws the dough against the bench and it makes a whoosh-slap sound. The dough separates into thin strands and he lobs them into a pot of boiling water. The noodles only need to cook for a minute before being tossed in a bowl with soy sauce, sticky fried spring onions, chopped coriander and lots of chilli oil. There's nothing like the texture of real hand-pulled noodles made from dough you just watched being flung high in the air: fresh, springy, each strand a slightly different size and shape.

There's also the dumpling shop run by two girls who wear matching orange caps. When I discovered their shengjian bao – fried soup dumplings – it was like an awakening. They are almost perfectly round, with a doughy but not-too-thick skin, filled with pork and chives and lots of hot soup, fried face-down for a thicker, crispier base. I eat them sitting at one of the rickety tables by the street, slitting open sachets of vinegar to pour over them.

But between the baozi stall and the shengjian shop is the most important one: bing. Bing is usually translated as 'pancake' or 'cake', but it really encompasses anything flat and round and edible, usually made with flour. The bing seller, perhaps in his thirties or forties, has soft lines around his eyes and wears a white cap on his head like many Hui Muslim people. Hui people come from north-western China, usually Gansu province or the Xinjiang autonomous region. I want to know more about him.

I want to know more about the breads and pancakes he sells, and where they come from. I try to start a conversation, but he is shy and uncommunicative, and before I can say anything meaningful I trip over my own words and lose confidence. The most I can do is ask 'What's this called?' and listen closely as he recites for me: jidan bing (savoury egg pancakes), zhima bing (sesame pancakes), lazhima bing (spicy sesame pancakes), pastries filled with red bean paste, and lots of other types of bing I haven't tried yet. The sesame pancakes are my favourite. A sesame pancake is like a savoury flatbread with a texture akin to roti canai when freshly made: crisp on the outside, chewy and fluffy on the inside. Layers of dough are stretched and folded on top of each other before being rolled out into a circle and fry-baked on something like a crêpe stone but with a lid. This gives the bing a flaky texture and crisp outer crust coated in crunchy sesame seeds. Soft, warm, golden. The taste of sesame oil and spring onions and a hint of garlic.

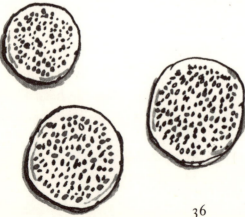

When I lived in Shanghai before, Mum used to bring sesame pancakes home from her weekend morning walks. We had big, lazy feasts at the kitchen table of fresh bing, sweet dried plums, steamed buns, and boiled dumplings with vinegar and soy sauce. We wrapped left-over pieces of sesame pancake in greaseproof paper and stored them in the freezer for midnight snacking.

This was the Shanghainese comfort food I missed the most after we left. I couldn't find any recipes (in English, at least) for this exact type of bing. The next closest thing was spring onion pancakes, cong youbing, the northern Chinese deep-fried equivalent. Sesame seeds didn't appear in any of the cong youbing recipes so I added them myself. I picked spring onions from my mother's garden, bought fresh yeast and good flour. I spent an afternoon kneading the dough, letting it rise, rolling it out, then folding and re-folding the corners of each layer on top of one another, like making those minia-ture origami fortune tellers we used to make at school. The resulting pancake was not like the real thing. It was dense, not light and fluffy, which meant too much time spent working the dough with my hands, not letting enough air in. I started again from the beginning.

￼

The homesick days of early spring are beginning to feel far away. I ride my bike through campus at night, when the frogs and cicadas are the loudest and the sky is purple and burnt orange. I stop to get a soft-serve ice cream and a box of strawberries so ripe they fall apart when I put them in my mouth. I run my fingers through my hair and flower stamens from the trees float to the floor. I lie on my bed in the afternoon when everything is slow and warm, my curtains billowing in the wind, making shapes in the soft light.

Now that it's June, I keep seeing friends online posting a quote from a poem by Anne Sexton – 'It is June. I am tired of being brave.' – from an elegy for her mother and father titled 'The Truth the Dead Know'. The poem is beautiful but it gets me down. It is June, I am in Shanghai and I am not tired. June in Shanghai is for cold bubble tea, for kissing, for three-yuan ice creams and misty rain mixing with sweat on skin. Another, less-quoted line in Sexton's poem reads 'When we touch we enter touch entirely'. I think this is the line this poem should be remembered for.

I wander back to class along Zhengsu Lu in the afternoon, my floral-print umbrella in one hand, an ice cream in the other. The air has that pre-lightning feel. It is June.

Sticky Rice Dumplings

粽子

I can feel sweat on the skin between my shoulder blades as I lean across the table to watch Chen Ayi's hands. She is showing me how to cut fresh lotus leaves into wide triangles like fans. When it's my turn, I grip the scissors and she guides me slowly upwards, following the grain of the thick leaves. They have a bitter, tea-like smell.

It is nearing the middle of a long, hot summer in Shanghai, with no classes and barely anyone around on the university campus. Most of my classmates have embarked on travels around Asia, to places still swelteringly hot but at least bearable, unlike Shanghai. I explain to other people that I don't have money for travel at the moment and besides, couldn't I use these eight weeks to get to know Shanghai better? A few months ago, the prospect of so much solitude would have been unthinkable. I welcome it now, although I am a little afraid of what it might to do me. So I put measures in place to keep myself busy. I go out at least once a day. I apply for a part-time tutoring job. I enrol on an online poetry course. I sign up for a cooking class specialising in home-style Cantonese cuisine.

I remember the humidity here from when I was a teen, but in my memory it's softer; less suffocating. Some days it's too hot to step outside for more than ten minutes at a time. The moment I leave my air-conditioned room and descend six flights of stairs into the wet heat, any small movement takes tremendous energy. My limbs become so heavy that walking feels more like swimming. My skin is permanently damp and sweat pools in the crinkles of my eyelids, stinging my eyes with salt. I squint into the distance and see shimmers of heat, all the colours melting together in waves.

Some days, I speak to no one except – briefly – baozi vendors and the friendly security guards outside the Foreign Students' Dormitory. I haven't touched another human being (being pushed up against strangers on the subway doesn't count) in three weeks. For a few days, I have a companion in the giant cicada that flies in through my window and sings loudly from beneath my bed. To me, this is the sound of a hot New Zealand summer by the sea. It doesn't belong here. I keep thinking the cicada has escaped, and then its piercing chime starts up again, calling and calling.

The other students in my cooking class are a mix of tourists and newly-arrived Shanghai residents. We are gathered in a semi-outdoor kitchen in the courtyard of a lanehouse somewhere deep in the Former French Concession. I wandered through plane trees to find it, sucking on a two-yuan Family Mart ice cream. A cheerful chef whose English name is Joey explains each part of the recipe, while a middle-aged woman called Chen Ayi does the actual cooking. She's not bothered by the fact that only two of us in the group can speak and understand Mandarin. She chatters away in a mixture of Shanghainese and Mandarin and Joey translates haltingly, struggling at times to keep up with her.

She is teaching us how to make the Cantonese version of what are known as zongzi in Shanghai: sticky rice dumplings wrapped in lotus leaves. She mixes cooked glutinous rice with pork fat, pieces of boneless chicken thigh and tiny dried shrimps. She forms lumps of the rice mixture into an oblong shape in her hands, then places it on the lotus leaf. She gently presses her fingers into the rice to make a well and spoons a duck egg yolk into the centre. Earlier we cracked the pale blue eggs into metal bowls. The plump yolks glowed bright orange on the bench like a row of suns. I note down how she wraps them, tucking excess folds of lotus leaf underneath. She places the parcels in the bamboo steamer, nestled close to each other. I am transfixed by her hands.

When it's my turn, I go slow. Wrapping zongzi in the stained leaves, folding the edges down and placing them in the steamer – it's just like making dumplings at home. It's a fiddly task that has a meditative rhythm. I always feel calmest and most in control when preparing dishes with my hands. All the sounds of my surroundings drop away. I feel the hot sun against my neck, and texture of the cold leaf in my palm.

Chen Ayi asks me what I do in Shanghai and where I live. When I mention I live alone, she seems to feel sorry for me and hands me three boxes of zongzi to take home. The following week I eat them for breakfast every day, sitting cross-legged on my balcony listening to Chinese indie rock. The gauzy curtains in the rooms across from me float up and down in the humid breeze. This trace of movement in the air makes it just about bearable to sit outside in the early morning. After the rich, salty zongzi, for something sweet I eat slices of fresh papaya bought from the fruit shop just outside the campus gate, ruby-coloured and shining like a gift.

◄◄◄

Every traditional Chinese festival has its special snacks. During Lunar New Year you have boiled dumplings, 'longevity noodles', whole steamed fish, and chewy glutinous rice cakes – niangao. At Tomb-Sweeping Festival there's tangyuan, green glutinous rice balls. And for Mid-Autumn Moon Festival, mooncakes. Zongzi belong to the Dragon Boat Festival, which falls on the fifth day of the fifth lunar month, usually in early June. The arrival of zongzi in the city – wrapped and folded en masse by Shanghainese families on street corners, piled high in bamboo steamers, and on display in supermarkets and corner shops – also signals the arrival of summer.

The Dragon Boat Festival commemorates the poet and government official Qu Yuan, who drowned himself in the Miluo River in 287 BC. It is said that people took their boats out onto the river and threw parcels of rice wrapped in leaves into the water to prevent fish from eating his body. In another version of the story, Qu Yuan becomes a water spirit. People threw rice into the river to feed his ghost, but the rice kept being eaten by a water dragon. The spirit of Qu Yuan returned to show them how to wrap the rice in river-soaked leaves so no water dragon would take it. Now we make dumplings in the shape of ox horns, pyramids, crescent moons and boats and birds.

Shanghai zongzi are a little larger than my fist, and wrapped in bamboo leaves rather than lotus. The long, flat strips are easier to form into the conical pyramid shape: you twirl the leaves into a cone in your hand, then pack it with the sticky rice filling. A mix of dark and light soy sauce turns the rice a rich brown. There are two main varieties of filling that can be mixed with the rice: sweet red bean or pork, often with an added duck egg yolk. The parcel gets tied up with string to hold it together, then it's boiled or steamed in a big pot or rice cooker. The bamboo leaves give off a deep, earthy scent that permeates the air throughout the end of May and early June.

It's the Cantonese variety, lo mai gai, that my mother always orders when we go for dim sum at the weekend. This kind is wrapped in a rectangular shape rather than the twirly pyramid. A cloud of steam erupts in the centre of the table as my mother leans forward to tenderly unwrap them with her chopsticks. The string already cut, she folds the leaves out one by one to reveal the steaming mound of fragrant chicken and sticky rice inside. She places a bit of chicken and rice into each of our bowls. As a child I was reluctant to try them, with their strange wet leaves and rich aroma. As an adult, the delicious smell won me over, along with everything it reminds me of: the sound of crowded dim sum restaurants, cups of jasmine tea, glowing custard tarts, my mother's hands moving plates around the table, and afterwards sucking on the peppermints that came with the bill.

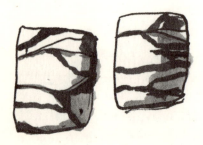

‹‹‹

粽

The first character of 粽子, zongzi, means 'pyramid-shaped dumpling made of glutinous rice, wrapped in bamboo or lotus leaves'. On the left-hand side of the character is the radical, the part that indicates meaning, which here is 米, mi: uncooked or unhusked rice. Put 米 together with 饭, fan, meaning 'meal', and you have mi-fan: steamed rice. On the right-hand side of the character is 宗 (zong), which indicates the sound. *Zong*. The end of the syllable sticks at the back of my throat. Incidentally, 宗 on its own means 'ancestor', or 'lineage'.

Long before my mother and grandmother taught me how to cook, they taught me how to eat. The way my mother separates papaya seeds from the fruit's flesh with her spoon, leaving a cluster of shiny black pearls. The way my grandmother peeled speckled quail eggs. How to wrench the heads off grilled prawns and suck the flesh from the shell, how to delicately peel off the white cheek from the head of a steamed fish, how to use your chopsticks and spoon together to pull noodles from one bowl to another, how to use your back teeth to crack the shell of a lychee. I learned by watching, then copying.

‹‹‹

Unlike tangyuan and mooncakes, which only appear in shops and bakery storefronts in the weeks leading up

45

to their corresponding festival, zongzi are abundant in Shanghai all year round. They are both a breakfast staple and an all-day snack. It was my friend and classmate Katrin who introduced me to a shop tucked away on campus that sold everything you could possibly need, including electric kettles, bedroom slippers, buckets and mops, shampoo, chocolate bars, vacuum-packed dried fish, and zongzi.

Katrin and I first met over noodles and crispy fried dumplings, near the end of my long, lonely summer. I was at my favourite cheap restaurant eating alone as usual, trying to finish as quickly as possible to avoid the large groups of newly-arrived students queueing up for their food. Foreign students always go out to eat and drink in packs. The new academic term was due to start next week and hordes of students were arriving day by day from all over the world, dissolving the eerie quiet that I'd grown used to in the dorm buildings. I already missed it. On some days, I'd been content with not speaking to anyone at all. But then Katrin approached and asked in English if she could sit at my empty table, and small talk by the steamed-up window came easily. We laughed together over our bowls of noodles, and I felt myself beginning to surface.

Weeks later, it's Katrin who brings me to the shop and points out the pyramid-shaped parcels soaking rather unappetisingly in a pot of brown liquid. Katrin goes for the sweet red-bean filled zongzi, her favourite; I choose the pork. The young woman behind the counter pulls out her scissors and makes a single snip into the strings and leaves, then tumbles the unfurled zongzi into a plastic bag. We thank her, hand over three yuan each, and stroll through campus towards the dorm buildings, batting mosquitoes and cicadas away as dusk falls.

◄◄◄

The weekend before term starts, I'm craving physical contact once more. I agree to meet up with a French boy with kind eyes who I met on Tinder. We sit on a bench by the Huangpu River, our elbows not quite touching. It's dark, except for some flashes of pink and green light. He's perfectly nice, but there's no attraction – but I'm bored and open to making friends, so I don't mind going with him to the river down by where he lives, a quiet spot just out of sight of Pudong's glittering skyline. We sit there talking and laughing, but I'm not fully aware of his presence. I am watching the lights rippling on the surface of the river and the windows in the buildings opposite intermittently flooding with colour. Glass skyscrapers tower above me; gold currents flash up and down their spines. I feel like I'm somewhere deep inside the city, almost close enough to touch its main artery. I'm not just floating through: I'm inside, looking out at the points where the city touches the clouds. I feel waves of colour on my skin.

I eventually detach myself from my date and hail a taxi, wanting to be back in my small room, alone. I ask the cab driver to drop me at Wujiaochang subway station, where I've parked my bike. I ride home in my yellow dress, pedalling fast down the main road that runs through campus, lined with fragrant ginko trees. It's past midnight but not fully dark. The trees glow yellow under the purple sky and there are pools of orange light pulsing out from the street lamps. For an urban campus in one of the biggest, busiest cities in the world, wild creatures flourish. At night in summertime, giant moths fly at the fluorescent bulbs and toads chirp rhythmically from the bushes on either side of the road. For a second I think I catch a glimpse of bats swarming and flapping around the treetops, though I think I might be dreaming.

My bike carves a thin trail through the sea of gingko leaves. I pause at the little shop on my way home – sometimes she's open late – and buy a zongzi for my midnight snack. The night is warm and heavy but I need something that will fill me, lull me to sleep. I take a few bites of the sticky rice before continuing on home.

Wonton Noodle Soup

馄饨面

I belong to a wonton-loving family. We eat them wherever we can around the world. One o'clock in the morning at a 24-hour dim sum restaurant in suburban Toronto; on Christmas Day at a shopping mall food court in Shanghai; at crowded eateries in Chinatowns across the world, in New York, Singapore, San Francisco, Auckland; in takeaways in Wellington; in airports; at street-side stalls in Kota Kinabalu; and at home on the couch, in front of the TV. No matter where I am, this is my way of returning home.

◄◄

The wonton, the dreamiest of all Chinese dumplings, goes by different names depending on the language or dialect. Here are three different Mandarin words that all mean 'wonton', along with their literal translations:

馄饨	huntun	irregular-shaped dumpling
云吞	yuntun	cloud swallow
抄手	chaoshou	to fold one's arms

I grew up with the delicate Cantonese kind, little round bundles of pork and shrimp (sometimes only shrimp) encased in a golden skin so thin it's semi-transparent. The joy is in the texture as much as the taste. Soft and slippery, they float on a bed of thin egg noodles in gingery soup. We eat them with plastic chopsticks in one hand and a spoon in the other. No sounds except occasional slurping, and the odd sigh.

China can be loosely divided into noodle territory and rice territory. Anywhere south of the Yangtze River is traditionally rice-growing country, where the climate is hotter and more humid, and the terrain mountainous. Rice usually accompanies main meals here, though noodles are often eaten for breakfast or as a snack. In the far north, where winter temperatures drop as low as minus thirty degrees, wheat-based carbohydrates and potatoes are the preferred staple food. Noodles, baked flatbreads and steamed bread buns abound. Situated at the point where the Yangtze River meets the East China Sea, Shanghai sits almost exactly in the middle. As a result, you get both. Shanghai is where two of the Eight Great Cuisines of China converge: the cuisines of Zhejiang Province and Jiangsu Province, both characterised by freshness, softness and lots of river fish and seafood dishes. Several times, Chinese friends took me to fancy Shanghainese restaurants where I tried some of the more famous Shanghai delicacies, such as the rich, meltingly sweet hongshao rou (red-braised pork), shizi tou ('lion's heads', which are in fact pork meatballs stuffed with vegetables), an array of pickled vegetables, river shrimps, and 'drunken chicken'. Once, the mother of a teenage girl I was tutoring in English insisted I take home a huge box of special xiaolongxia, literally 'little dragon shrimps', a kind of spiky crayfish local to Shanghai whose shells turn blood red when cooked. In spite of these renowned Shanghainese delicacies, it's the street snacks that have always excited me most. I would choose a comforting bowl of wontons over red-braised pork any day.

I've learnt that the skins of dumplings get thicker the further north you travel. As you head south, dumplings become delicate and translucent. Shanghai specialises in both. Shanghai wontons are less famous than their Cantonese counterparts and are rarely found outside of China, but they're distinctive. Da huntun, 'big wontons', are heavy and hearty, filled with pork and chives rather than shrimp. But my favourite kind are xiao huntun, so small that you could eat several in one mouthful. Just a dollop of pork and ginger enveloped in a thicker dough made from flour, egg, salt and water, similar to the consistency of handmade pasta. I think they look like little princesses dressed in oversized gowns.

For a quick and comforting breakfast, lunch, dinner or a snack in between, I go straight to my favourite diner on the corner of my street. I pay six yuan for a bowl of twelve and slurp them down while reading my book. They arrive floating gracefully in a bowl of light broth, with strips of omelette and diced spring onion sprinkled into the soup. I leave feeling stronger, warmer and more myself.

Specialty wonton shops can be found all over Shanghai. They are always small establishments, three or four tables at most, with stools spilling out onto the sidewalk in spring and summer. The menu is often printed in bright green on the wall of the shop, with little variation: pork wontons, pork and chive wontons, pork and mushroom wontons, or small wontons with pork and ginger only. Add noodles for an extra two yuan, and add your own chilli oil and vinegar at each table. They are steamy, quiet places amidst the din of the city. Just the sound of coins hitting the side of the change bowl, some slurping, and maybe a gentle humming from the person who sits there folding every single wonton by hand, usually a young woman.

I breathe in the smell of ginger and spring onions that wafts out onto the streets of Shanghai late into the night. At a wonton shop just outside the university gates, I watch a mother and daughter making them in the back corner. First a square-shaped wrapper held in the palm, then a teaspoonful of pork in the centre, then it's squeezed shut. They work at a rate of about one wonton every three seconds, all while taking customers' orders and watching a reality TV show on the iPad propped up on the table between them. The women's hands move so fast their fingers become a blur.

◀◀

In late June I take a trip to Hong Kong on my own. Christina, a friend from Wellington whom I've known since school, is passing through Hong Kong Airport for a day and I decide on a whim to spend most of my scholarship allowance for the month on cheap flights and a hostel for a few days.

When I arrive, I resist the urge to retreat to my hostel with a book. I try to remember that eating alone in Shanghai is one of my favourite things; it should be the same in Hong Kong, too. I am in the land where pineapple buns were invented, along with so many of my other favourite things that remind me of home. I find a noodle shop next to a giant shopping mall. Like all the best noodle shops, the place is small and crowded and everything happens fast, but I notice that there's slightly more elbow room than in other places where only locals go, perhaps to make tourists and expats feel a little more at ease – but you're still sharing a tables with an uncle and auntie and grandpa, just as it should be. I order shrimp wonton noodle soup with a side plate of steamed gai lan. These are the only two items on the menu. The wontons are slippery clouds with pale golden tails floating in broth that is so delicious and fortifying it sends pulses of warmth directly to my core. The egg noodles are thin and crinkly, just how I like them, and hard to get a good grip on with chopsticks. I eat quickly and noisily, crunching on the green gai lan stems.

Afterwards, I step out onto the street and watch the two male chefs through the window. One for noodles, one for dumplings. They are deep in concentration, assembling bowls of soup and lifting ladlefuls of wontons into each with practiced precision. After dinner I stop at a bakery and buy two golden-yellow pineapple buns with warm custard inside. I put one in my backpack for tomorrow's breakfast.

AUTUMN

season of persimmons, green mandarins
& pink-flesh honey pomelo

Breakfast in Shanghai
上海早饭

What I eat for breakfast in Shanghai depends on the season, my mood, and the level of rainfall.

On a cold, smoggy morning, I have a cup of pu'er tea in my bedroom and two baozi from the lady at the baozi shop who has red cheeks. I take off my gloves and peel the thin paper from each bun's round bottom. The steam burns my fingers and my lips.

For a warm morning in late spring, I eat boiled dumplings with chilli oil and half a pink-fleshed pomelo, a bigger, sweeter kind of grapefruit. I'm learning the words for new kinds of fruit almost every day, just like when I was little and there were cheerful cut-outs of apples, pears and oranges and their corresponding characters on the walls of the classroom at my Saturday morning Chinese classes. 柚子, honey pomelo; 柿子, persimmon; 青梅, green plum. Holding the pomelo in place on my desk, I pierce the skin with a knife and split it slowly, listening to the soft ripping sound of the flesh pulling away from the rind.

The morning after a summer downpour, I order a bowl of silken tofu at a 24-hour eatery. The layers float in swirls of soy sauce like a chrysanthemum flower in a pot of tea. Every mouthful of this doufu hua – 'beancurd flower' – slips down in one swallow. The tofu is topped with spring onions, coriander, chilli flakes and dried shrimps.

When I am longing for home, I make a cup of peppermint tea in my room. I eat Chinese yoghurt topped with a handful of German-imported muesli that I bought from the foreign supermarket, out of my pink melamine noodle bowl I brought with me all the way from Wellington.

On a yellow autumn morning, in a hurry to get to class, it has to be jianbing. Jianbing is the famous Shanghainese breakfast wrap, consisting of a thin eggy crepe wrapped around a fried dough stick, Chinese sausage, some lettuce and coriander, a sheet of crispy wonton skin and a layer of salty-sweet bean paste. It's the sauce that makes it special. I watch the jianbing maker dip her brush into the chocolate-coloured paste and spread it on the pancake in wide circles. She asks, 'Yao la ma?' *Do you want it spicy?* I shake my head. She rolls it up and passes it to me. I stand and eat half on the street next to my bike, where leaves from the plane trees are beginning to gather in piles. I wrap the other half up and put it in my coat pocket for later. For the rest of the morning I can feel the weight of it in my pocket, a small parcel of warmth close to my body.

‹‹‹

小吃

Xiaochi are the lifeblood of Shanghai. 小吃, xiaochi, can be loosely translated as 'snacks', but this doesn't seem to cover it. The literal meaning of the word is 'small eats'. More substantial than a snack yet smaller than a meal. This encompasses all the hot, savoury street food offerings of Shanghai: fried dumplings, wontons with sesame paste, small bowls of noodles, zongzi, spring onion pancakes. Xiaochi are very much unique to each city. People make special trips to try the biang biang noodles of Xi'an, the flatbreads of Xinjiang or the famous 'crossing-the-bridge rice noodles' of Yunnan province. 'Xiaochi' means something you could eat in the late afternoon to stave off hunger, or late at night after coming home from a karaoke party with your classmates. Anything you could make a meal out of simply by ordering a double portion, which I found myself doing most days.

Every night at ten o'clock, street vendors and their carts line the stretch of road just outside the university gates. They will stay there almost all through the night or until the police appear, which happens once a week or so, causing them to scatter and regroup further down Wudong Lu. They are in prime position to greet the crowds of drunken students returning from their nights out. The air is thick with steam and smoke and the smell of barbecued meat.

‹‹‹

Breakfast at the university cafeteria features a choice of savoury items: soup noodles, congee, dumplings, doufu hua, steamed baozi with many different fillings, flatbreads and fried pancakes. Two baozi, one sweet and one savoury, is the classic student breakfast here. They can be eaten on the bus or on the way to class, steering your bike with one hand through the tree-lined streets.

One morning I receive a WeChat message from Louise: 'Have you tried this fried egg pancake thing at canteen? Like roti but better. Game changer.' Louise is also a New Zealander, and fully understands my love of breakfast. We arrived in Shanghai on the same day back in February, cold and bewildered. She walks so fast I can't keep up with her and has big blue eyes that glow with warmth and laughter.

The cafeteria meals are decent and incredibly cheap, which means we spend considerably more time here at the end of each month, when our scholarship stipend begins to dwindle. After a few months we've tried everything, so when something new appears behind the canteen counter, especially at breakfast, it's worth messaging about.

The next morning I approach the bing counter and see that Louise is right. A new variety of Shanghainese pancake has appeared, made of light, flaky, paratha-like dough with a bonus egg fried into the pancake. Under normal circumstances I might think better of eating something so greasy for breakfast, but my year of studying in Shanghai is almost over and I know I may never again possess such a high tolerance for rich, oily snacks this early in the morning. Now is the time. I scan my lunch card on the card reader and offer up my plastic tray. The egg pancake is a warm, delicious mess. It's the ultimate comforting breakfast: crisp, chewy, salty and soft on the inside. It reminds me of the hand-rolled roti canai I used to buy from the south Indian takea-way in Kelburn, up in the green hills above Wellington, a few minutes' walk from my flat.

⦅⦅

It's autumn in Shanghai. In the streets I spy small islands made of wet leaves, birds in cages hanging above doorways and balconies, escaped white balloons floating high above the city, and a gift shop that sells glass bottles with live goldfish inside. I learn a new word: xian, an archaic word for wildfires. 'Xian' pronounced in different tones can also mean fresh, bright, a light yellow, silkworm, and to hunt in autumn. The city is changing colour. The city is turning. In September, mooncake season coincides with typhoon season. Cold rain pours off the edge of highway bridges, hitting the tops of buses and taxis with a loud rushing sound. Little dogs wear raincoats and matching rain boots. There are people on the crowded subway with sodden boxes of mooncakes cradled in their arms.

Mid-Autumn Festival, also known as the Moon Festival, falls on the fifteenth day of the eighth lunar month each year. Instead of going out drinking with our class-mates at one of many student dive bars down the road, Louise and I are tasting yuebing – mooncakes. Moon-cakes come in an infinite variety of fillings and flavours, some individually wrapped in green, blue and pink plastic packaging, their ingredient lists full of words we've not yet learned. Earlier that day, at our local supermarket, we braved the mooncake bins where you pick your own selection and pay by weight. I had my phone to hand, looking up un-known characters on my dictionary app. Lotus seeds, almond paste, strawberry-flavoured essence. Mooncakes are usually very dense and sweet, with a ball of filling inside – often red bean paste or lotus seed paste or peanuts and a whole egg yolk.

They can also be savoury: the traditional Shanghai version is made of flaky pastry and has minced pork inside, not unlike a Cornish pasty. We buy a selection of the strangest looking ones. Sitting on my balcony, just big enough for two, we catch the last of the summer's warmth and sit overlooking a sea of identical dormitory buildings, lights in the windows flickering off and on as violet dusk washes over the city. We cut the mooncakes into quarters with a plastic knife and lay them on paper plates between us. The rose-flavoured cake reminds me of pot pourri and shampoo. The matcha and taro cake decorated with green and violet swirls is the one we like best. 'This one tastes like grass,' says Louise, making a face, and we curl up in laughter. Her laugh is one of the best sounds I know.

◀◀

On an October evening I am in Maggie's kitchen at her apartment in Pudong, over an hour's subway journey from where I live. Maggie was born in Shanghai and is a close friend of my mother. She's known me since I was twelve. We are pouring pancake batter directly into a large wok coated in vegetable oil. I am watching closely and taking notes on my phone. I ask for measurements but there are none; this is simply Maggie's version of egg pancakes, jidan bing, something she has always known how to cook. There are just four ingredients: four large eggs, a little flour, a little salt, and finely chopped spring onions (only the green parts). The wok's flame heats up the whole kitchen and makes every room in the house fragrant. With Maggie's husband and her father-in-law, we eat them fresh from the wok, crisp at the edges, with garlicky bok choi, Shanghai river prawns and a little steamed rice. Maggie's father-in-law shuts his eyes as he takes a bite. He says they're just like how his mother made them when he was a child. Later, I write up Maggie's recipe on my laptop.

◀◀

In another city, in another country, I search through my emails for Maggie's recipe that I sent to my mother many months ago. Subject line: *The best bing I've ever had*. In the morning, I pull spring onions from the small patch growing in a corner of my parents' garden, beneath the jasmine that is just beginning to flower. I crack four eggs into a bowl, add a cup of flour, a little water, a little salt, and mix them together with the sort of ladle meant for scooping rice from the bottom of the pot. I heat oil in the wok and watch for smoke. I pour ladlefuls of yellowy pancake mix into the pan, a thin layer, and watch the edges begin to crisp. When it turns to pure gold, I use chopsticks to lay the pancake on a blue enamel plate, one of many my mother brought back from her own mother's kitchen in Kota Kinabalu. I eat them by the window overlooking the sea.

Chinese Aubergines

茄子

In November there are crushed leaves on the streets of Shanghai. In Yangshuo, there are crushed butterflies.

Yangshuo is a small town in China's near-tropical Guangxi autonomous region. Katrin and I are biking along a dusty road that curves between rice paddy fields and vegetable crops. On either side of us, rows of karst mountains stretch for miles. This distinctive jagged landscape is made of limestone, dolomite and gypsum, with deep caves and tunnels hidden beneath the mountains. The same formations can be found in other parts of Southeast Asia, such as Thailand and Vietnam. Here, the rocky shapes are coated in shrubs and semi-tropical trees. Butterflies and birds fling themselves out of the dark green forest and the gravel road is dotted with vibrant roadkill: butterflies with orange and white wings, royal purple wings, pale yellow-green wings.

Yangshuo Cooking School is nestled in a corner of rural Chaolong Village, next to apricot trees and a vegetable patch. Pink bougainvillea flowers creep over the garden walls. This afternoon, Katrin and I are the only students. Head chef Sophie, who is the same age as me and grew up in Yangshuo, teaches us how to cook steamed chicken with goji berries, pork and mint dumplings, and stir-fried aubergine with ginger and garlic. Accustomed to holding classes mainly for English-speaking tourists, Sophie delights in being able to teach us mostly in Mandarin, with Katrin and I asking her to repeat phrases every now and then. I use the heel of my palm and my cleaver to crush several fat cloves of garlic in quick succession, feeling their skins burst. Back in Shanghai, with no real kitchen in my dormitory, I rarely cook. I had forgotten the joy of smashing something to pieces in a single blow. I had forgotten how good it is to make things with my hands, and how much I need it. All other sounds and sensations begin to disappear. There is nothing but the sound of our cleavers chopping chives and fresh chillies, and the feel of peeling gnarled pieces of ginger between my fingers. Wary of too much heat, I want to use only half a chilli but Sophie convinces me to add the whole thing. 'Go on – you can take more than you think,' she says.

A basket of qiezi, Chinese aubergines, sits by the door leading out to the vegetable garden. They are long and skinny with bright violet skin, different to the ones in supermarkets back home. The texture of the flesh is a little denser than the aubergines I'm used to – less spongy. We cook thick purple-skinned pieces in the wok with chopped ginger and garlic until they are soft, almost melting, just held together by the skin. The open-air kitchen smells of rice wine and ginger, just like my mother's kitchen and my grandmother's, too. I look up from my wok after what feels like a long time and see the mountains on the other side of the valley turning blue.

◀◀

Guangxi is a mountainous, semi-tropical region of southern China. It became one of China's five 'autonomous regions' in 1958, along with Tibet, Inner Mongolia, Xinjiang and Ningxia. Many Chinese ethnic minority groups live in the Guangxi region, especially the Zhuang people. The region shares a border with Vietnam and is teeming with rice paddies and lush forest, so Guangxi food is light, fresh and a little bit spicy. Rice, rice cakes and rice noodles are abundant, as are bamboo leaves and game meat.

It's our mid-semester break and we are here for just four days, a brief escape from the damp winter cold descending on Shanghai. The night train to Guilin, the nearest big city to Yangshuo, takes seventeen hours. I bring a separate bag for snacks for the journey. Taking the night train feels fun and adventurous so long as you're with friends and don't mind peeing into a hole in the train floor through which you can catch glimpses of the railway tracks moving beneath. There are six bunks to every open-plan 'cabin', and a snack trolley does the rounds every few hours: six flavours of cup noodles, vacuum-packed dried fish, dried chicken feet, Pringles, Oreos, salted nuts, tins of soy milk and Chinese sausages so pink they appear luminous. For dinner, we pour boiling water into Styrofoam cups and watch our noodles plump up in the steam.

Long distance trains are a regular part of life for many people who can't afford to fly and whose hometowns are far away. Noodles are the only hot meal available on such long journeys, so eating cup noodles on a night train seems to be a time-honoured ritual. At the station, almost every person at the platform is carrying multiple packs of noodles, either poking out of their luggage or in plastic bags tied to their packs. On the train I walk past families clutching Styrofoam bowls and wooden chopsticks, steam puffing out from beneath the paper lids. The rhythmic sound of the train is accompanied with a chorus of slurps. I wonder if, for some, cup noodles' colourful plastic packaging is synonymous with travel. From my top bunk, I watch the elderly couple in the bunks below us cut cubes of boiled eggs they brought from home into their noodle cups. The woman takes out two jars, adding a spoonful each of homemade pickled veggies and chilli oil into the soup. Afterwards, they pour out cups of black tea from a glass flask. I wonder where they're going, and where they call home.

The world outside the train darkens and we settle into our bunks. If I crane my neck backwards I can just see out of the window beneath me. A parade of pylons, factories, power stations and elevated highways. As dusk falls, we cross into unknown territory for me. I feel uneasy; I am not used to being so far from the sea. Shanghai's glowing river and record-breaking skyscrapers feel like a faraway dream. But the city's fluorescent neons linger on: the flat landscape is illuminated by giant characters glowing from low buildingtops in shimmering red and yellow and green. The train is moving too fast for me to read them all but I catch flashes of words I recognise: 日 sun, 明 bright, 健康 healthy, 电 electric, 月 moon. I think of how so many words in Chinese are made up of separate, strangely poetic components which make up the word's full meaning. A computer (电脑) is an electric brain; an avocado (鳄梨 or 牛油果) is an alligator pear or butter fruit; a film (电影) an electric shadow.

The two characters of 桂林, Guilin, together mean 'sweet osmanthus forest'. In November, the region lives up to its name and all the roads are covered in dainty white and yellow osmanthus flowers. Guilin is surrounded by the same dramatic mountains as Yangshuo but it has become a noisy, dusty, bustling city. Yangshuo, a short bus ride away along the picturesque Li River, was once a sleepy town and is now a tourism hotspot. The scenery of Yangshuo, known in China as 'the brightest place on earth', is depicted on the back of the twenty yuan note.

I first visited when I was thirteen, on a school trip organised by my international school in Shanghai. I mostly remember drinking mango smoothies every day, trekking through the hills, swimming in the Li River and wandering down the cobbled main street, spotting dragonflies. Yangshuo is different now, no longer a quiet oasis, with nightclubs and bars and virtual reality arcades glittering beneath the limestone hills. But if I clung to these places as they are in my memories, I'd soon have nowhere left to return.

◄◄◄

The path is deserted. Somehow, despite reading online about the 'near-vertical climbs' and 'iron ladders in some places', I am here on the side of a small mountain called Laozhai Shan. Three of my friends bound on ahead of me, following the steep path that hugs the mountain.

It's dark and cool beneath the canopy of leaves. Trees have been cleared at points along the path to make way for concrete graves with plastic flowers laid on top. Some also have also mangoes, oranges, burnt-out incense sticks. It reminds me of the cemetery we always pass on our way from the airport in Kota Kinabalu, where graves painted blue, pink and orange are set deep into the hillside, draped in wreaths of chrysanthemums and bowls of fruit.

The climb is short, despite the steepness. After about forty minutes, the trees begin to clear and we scramble over uneven rocks on our hands and knees to reach the peak. I am the last to pull myself up, blood rushing in my ears. Suddenly we are surrounded by a vast sky and, below us, a sea of mountains. Between them curves the Li River, now appearing in miniature. There are butterflies with blue wings that catch the light, and hornets the size of dragonflies. We stand in the shade of a little red pagoda that has been built on the cliff edge. Gradually, while the butterflies fly close to our faces, breath begins to return to our bodies.

Back down at the foot of the mountain, we buy a kilo of mandarins from the ladies selling fruit and supplies at a stall by the road. For a late lunch, we stop at the first little restaurant we can find and order several plates of Guilin rice noodles, six yuan each. This is the most famous xiaochi in Guilin: plain fresh rice noodles, similar to the type of noodles that are a staple in Vietnamese cuisine, topped with chilli flakes, pickled bamboo shoots, green beans, pickled soy beans, spring onions, fried peanuts (optional for those allergic to nuts, like me) and your choice of meat. There is something about rice noodles that makes them my ultimate comfort food. Maybe it's their softness and chewiness, their luminous white colour, the way they absorb flavour. When I eat them I remember pulling apart fat, sticky strands of Cantonese hofun noodles with my chopsticks when I was little, chewing on them one by one. We also order braised aubergine, similar to the dish Sophie taught us how to prepare at

Yangshuo Cooking School. Shades of vibrant purple shine through the thick, dark sauce. It's nothing complicated: a combination of light and dark soy sauce, vinegar, garlic and ginger tossed with thick pieces of aubergine that have been fried until soft, almost sweet. I can hear the distant crackle of firecrackers in the distance, signalling a wedding or a joyous family get-together somewhere nearby.

Katrin and I bike home in the late afternoon, our legs aching and our bellies full. I spot another butterfly resting in the sun on a fencepost, small with orange wings that have black and purple spots on them. The road is littered with the charred casings of exploded firecrackers. Katrin's semester abroad is coming to an end and she'll be travelling home to Germany soon. She tells me she's ordered a packet of seeds online on Taobao so she can grow her own Chinese aubergines in her garden at home. I find this both hilarious and inspiring.

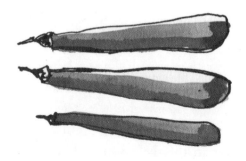

We already know that it's the food we'll miss the most when we leave China, and we are preparing ourselves for it with plenty of cooking classes, culinary research and, in Katrin's case, a bit of stockpiling.

‹‹‹

On our last day in Yangshuo I make one last trip to The Mango Tree, the cafe we've been visiting every day. Every item on the menu contains mango: mango ice cream, mango yoghurt, mango juice, mango shaved ice. I sit on the tiny upstairs balcony eating a Hong Kong-style bubble waffle topped with vanilla ice cream and cubes of fresh mango. I write postcards to people I haven't spoken to in a long time. I also write a list. I've begun to notice that one way of tracking the changing seasons in Shanghai is by looking at the fruit that's most abundant in the markets:

late winter: tiny sweet mandarins

spring: seedless green grapes

late spring: papaya, nashi pears

midsummer: watermelons, watermelons, watermelons

late summer: pineapples, nectarines, black plums

autumn: bright red persimmons, green mandarins

late autumn: honey pomelo

Sitting in my bunk on the train with a pink honey pomelo from my snack bag, I make another list:

<u>Places where reality feels altered</u>

never-ending escalators with mirrors above them

campus at night, full of animal noises and soft colours

wide avenues surrounded by empty apartment blocks

Walmart at closing time

empty subway trains full of fluorescent light

empty subway platforms just before the last train leaves

overnight trains

These used to make me feel lonely, but they don't anymore. They are all places of temporary existence – of waiting, coming and going – where you aren't meant to stand still. In this city you're supposed to keep moving, but I let myself be still. I go for long walks in the evening and watch other people in their private solitude. Everything around me is disappearing and reappearing at the same time and I will never be able to keep up, and for the moment I know that's okay. I can't stop the city from changing shape, but by writing things down – recipes, names, colours, Chinese characters – I can hold it still for a moment. I can mark my existence here, now.

◀◀

At half past eleven each day, hordes of students spill out of lecture halls towards the cafeteria. You need to be fast if you want to get to the front of the queue. With our Chinese classes always at least a ten-minute walk from the cafeteria, we are never, ever fast enough. The huge dining hall contains over twenty kiosks, where students and professors alike join the queues that snake between the tables, everyone holding red and orange plastic trays. There's no time for indecision; once you're at the front, you'd better know what you want. There are fewer people in the so-called 'Western Canteen' on the far side of the hall, where pizza and salads and steaks can be bought for almost three times the price of the Chinese meals. Louise and I head straight upstairs to our favourite area: the Halal canteen. Here, the cooks and servers are all from China's prominent Muslim ethnic groups, mostly Hui or Uyghur, originating in northwestern China. The food is Halal and much of it is vegetarian. There's cumin-spiced lamb kebabs, pilaf-like rice dishes, pork-free mapo tofu, freshly baked flatbreads, and most famously, niurou mian – beef noodle soup. The noodles are hand-pulled to order by noodle makers who work directly behind the kiosk counter. The whirling and slapping sound of them pulling the dough reverberates across the dining hall.

The dishes here change every day or so, but lately our favourite has been making a regular appearance: aubergine stir-fried until meltingly soft in a garlicky, gingery sauce. Sometimes there's tomatoes and chillies thrown in, sometimes not. Spoon in one hand, chopsticks in the other, I devour mine with rice and side dishes of dry-fried green beans and tender steamed pumpkin.

Some students, locals included, say that the cafeteria food is too salty and greasy, and they can't bear it for longer than three days in a row. At the back of our minds we know that eating like this every day can't possibly be good for us, but we're only here for so long. We may never taste anything like this soft, meaty aubergine again. We mop up the last of the fried garlic and purple aubergine skin with pieces of flatbread still warm from the stone oven. Twenty minutes later, it's time to head back to class or we risk being late. I bike one-handed back to the other side of campus, an important skill I've picked up over this past year, stopping at a Family Mart along the way. The familiar jingle rings out constantly from above the door as students crowd inside for last-minute snacks. I choose a mini pot of strawberry ice cream from the fridge by the counter, the kind that comes with a fold-up spoon hidden under the lid. I have a few moments left to myself before class starts. I linger by a crabapple tree near the tall statue of Mao Zedong that overlooks the WestGate. I think of Katrin's aubergine plants slowly growing in her back garden in Frankfurt, bearing fruit almost a year later and for years to come, bright purple treasures from far away.

WINTER AGAIN

season of oranges, pomegranates

Boiled Dumplings
饺子

My life with dumplings began in a crowded restaurant with jade-green walls. It smelled like meat and jasmine tea. Clinking porcelain, guttural shouts, chopsticks clattering onto the tiled floor. Old women with very few teeth pushed carts piled high with bamboo steamers. I pointed at what I wanted to eat: three dumplings and a 7-Up, please. Mum had taught me the names but I was always too shy to speak Chinese. As usual I ate the outside part, the slippery skin, my favourite part of the dumpling. Then I sheepishly tipped the filling into my dad's bowl. Bored of sitting still, I slid off my seat and wound my way past the carts and tables to the front window where three big lobsters snoozed in a tank of cloudy water. We always left with a box of mooncakes wrapped in red tissue paper, and a handful of peppermints.

◄◄◄

It is said that jiaozi, boiled dumplings, began as a cure for frostbite. In the middle of a harsh northern winter almost two thousand years ago, a Chinese physician named Zhang Zhongjing made little dough parcels filled with lamb, chilli, ginger and garlic, folded them in the shape of an ear, cooked them in boiling water, and fed them to those suffering from the cold. He called them 嬌耳 jiao'er – tender ears.

All over China, jiaozi are eaten for every meal and every snack in between, but ten times more than usual are consumed on the eve of the Lunar New Year. The communal act of making dumplings represents the family coming together, something that might only happen once a year, with the mass exodus of young people from rural villages to the cities. If you look into people's windows just before midnight, you'll see them shaping balls of dough into discs in the palms of their hands, laying them out on the table in a row, then filling and folding them in the traditional crescent shape. The grandma might fix up the wonky ones so they don't burst open in the boiling water. The steamed-up windows almost shut out the light of fireworks shooting across the building tops.

‹‹‹

The beginning feels far away now. I remember the feeling of eating alone for the first time in Shanghai, a few days after I arrived. The idea seemed unbearable but the alternative was eating alone in my room. I could at least go outside, leave the confines of campus and join the noise and colours of the city. I forced myself to say to the

cashier: 'Zheli chi, xiexie.'
I'll eat in, thank you.
Congyou banmian and
a bowl of mini wontons.
There was a young student
slurping noodles opposite
me, totally immersed in her
e-book. She looked startled
when I asked if she could pass
me the soy sauce, but did so
with a half-smile. When I raised
my arm to take the sticky bottle
from her, our palms almost touched.

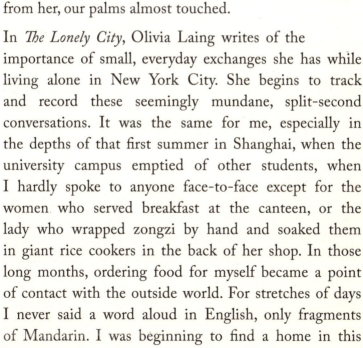

In *The Lonely City*, Olivia Laing writes of the importance of small, everyday exchanges she has while living alone in New York City. She begins to track and record these seemingly mundane, split-second conversations. It was the same for me, especially in the depths of that first summer in Shanghai, when the university campus emptied of other students, when I hardly spoke to anyone face-to-face except for the women who served breakfast at the canteen, or the lady who wrapped zongzi by hand and soaked them in giant rice cookers in the back of her shop. In those long months, ordering food for myself became a point of contact with the outside world. For stretches of days I never said a word aloud in English, only fragments of Mandarin. I was beginning to find a home in this language, one shared by my mother and her family but here and now, at this exact point in time, occupied only by me. The language was a lifeline, an opening, and eating alone became a silent ritual.

My last meal in Shanghai that final winter is a small plate of jiaozi filled with pork and Chinese cabbage, with a basket of chewy, flaky spring onion pancakes. As usual, I am eating by myself. It helps that in this city there are likely thousands of people or even hundreds of thousands eating their bowl of noodles or dumplings alone at any given moment. For a short while, I am one of them.

Dongbei Feng is a northern-style Chinese restaurant inside a shopping mall in Wujiaochang, the busy shopping area within walking distance from campus. Students, both local and foreign, are everywhere. In the months leading up to my departure, they've begun demolishing the buildings that contain my beloved food-court restaurants. Dongbei Feng still stands, as does the place where I go to eat my favourite spring onion noodles, but not for long. If I come back to visit in a year's time, Wujiaochang will be unrecognisable. This phenomenon is nothing new – since the late 1980s, when China opened up to the West and began its rapid race to modernisation, shiny new shopping malls and residential developments are being built all the time, squeezing out the old street vendors and small traders. "Old" malls built ten years ago are now being replaced by newer, bigger ones; the city is constantly building and re-building itself. New xiaochi food streets and food courts re-emerge all the time. In a year's time, students will simply flock elsewhere for their cheap dumpling fix.

These are the dumplings I grew up with. Seconds ago they were ladled from the pot of boiling water onto my plate, still steaming and glistening, their pearly white skins a little wonky and uneven: a reassuring sign that the dough has been rolled by hand, not machine. The pork and cabbage filling is seasoned with ginger, spring onions and soy sauce, with an egg to bind the mix together. Sometimes also a little sesame oil, five-spice or MSG powder, depending on whose secret recipe it is. Dedicated dumpling restaurants such as this one serve delicious vegetarian options too: egg and chives, egg and tomato (a particularly northern combination), mushroom and chives. On the table, there are always three condiments in porcelain jars: soy sauce, black vinegar and chilli oil.

Jiaozi remind me of helping my mother in our steam-filled kitchen at home by the sea. They remind me of the cold, dark month I spent studying in Beijing when I was nineteen, the sun permanently clouded by a thick haze of pollution, living off jiaozi every morning and evening. When I ordered them to takeaway, I received black vinegar in a little plastic bag tied shut with a rubber band. Extra chilli oil for extra cold, homesick afternoons. What does it mean to taste something and be transported to so many places at once, all of them a piece of home? To be half-elsewhere all the time, half-here and not-here. There are two sides of myself: one longing for the city, one at peace near the sea.

◄◄

I will never be ready to say goodbye to Shanghai, so I don't. When it's time to leave, I take with me as much as I can carry. Winter in Shanghai will soon give way to summer in Wellington. This is, for me, as natural as the changing of the seasons.

I take dumplings with me wherever I go. The summer after leaving, I visit Katrin at her home in Frankfurt and we fold jiaozi together at her small kitchen table, using an vegan filling of chopped aubergines, mushrooms, tofu, spring onions and spinach. Next I fly to San Francisco, where Jessie and Karen live – we've been friends since middle school in Shanghai. We stroll together through San Francisco's Chinatown to buy ingredients: shiitake mushrooms, fresh tofu, bok choi, ginger. I step inside a shop crammed with Chinese kitchen utensils. There are paper lanterns hanging from every bit of ceiling and strings of lights coiled around the doorways. I point to a brilliant blue cloth lantern I want to bring home with me and hang in my bedroom. It's her last one, the shopkeeper tells me, and all covered in dust, so it's only ten dollars. She smiles. The pattern of yellow and pink peonies against blue is almost identical to Maggie

Cheung's cheongsam in *In the Mood for Love*, that slow-burning, blue-tinted film. The tenement buildings are painted green and pink and blue and gold. Groups of aunties and grandmas congregate on every corner chatting in Hakka and Cantonese, their shopping bags full of chives and melons and daikon. In any city anywhere, if there's a Chinatown I'll feel at home.

We fold our jiaozi on Jessie's bedroom floor in her shared apartment on Polk Street. It's muscle memory by now: I dip my fingers in a little water and dab it around the edge of the dough to make a glue, place a teaspoon of filling in the centre of the circle, fold it into a half circle and make six to eight folds along the rim, squeezing the dough between my thumb and forefinger. We fall into a familiar rhythm, the silence broken occasionally by fits of laughter. We have each been taught this skill a long time ago – by mothers, sisters, friends – and it connects us to a place both real and unreal, a home that no longer exists but is preserved in memory. I place little dishes of soy sauce and vinegar between the bowls of dumplings and we have a picnic on the floor, lilac San Francisco sunset clouds shifting in the sky beyond.

◄◄

When I chance upon a Chinese grocer's or any Asian supermarket anywhere in the world, I fall into a trance. I sway in front of aisles packed with a hundred different brands of instant noodles. I become giddy at the sight of all the snacks my mother loves: the dried plums in bright purple packets, rice crackers, dried peas, pungent vacuum-packed salted cuttlefish. I resist the urge to stroke the green-gold papayas and mangoes. I head for the freezer section, where the dumpling skins are stacked according to national variety: for Korean mandu, for Japanese gyoza, for Tibetan momos. In London's Chinatown in the middle of winter I once bought a kumquat tree, just because they were there, and because my parents had a kumquat tree on the balcony of one of the many houses I grew up in. In her essay "Crying in H Mart", the American musician and writer Michelle Zauner, who is of Korean descent, describes her local Korean supermarket as a kind of sanctuary and magic portal. Sitting in a Korean food court in suburban Philadelphia, she wonders who else around her is missing home. What memory are they reliving? Where are they trying to reach? Who are they desperately trying not to forget? If she saw me, she might know.

Where I live now, the nearest Asian supermarket is a bus and a train ride away. This means I must teach myself to make my own dough for the jiaozi pi, dumpling skins,

82

something I always thought was beyond me – a skill reserved only for the most experienced Chinese aunties and grandmas.

The first time I try, I'm cooking for one. There are only two ingredients: flour and water. I make a well in the flour with a spoon and add lukewarm water. Different recipes call for different temperatures: cold water makes for a stiff dough, making it better for fried dumplings; hot or just-boiled water creates a softer, more malleable texture, better for sealing the jiaozi edges tightly before boiling. The family-run website that I rely on for most Chinese recipes, The Woks of Life, calls for less water in humid climates. Fuchsia Dunlop in *Every Grain of Rice* calls for cold water. I choose blood temperature. Rain streams down the kitchen skylight.

The dough is soft and pliant. I pull the ball into two halves and then in half again. I roll them into cylinders and cut them into small gnocchi-like chunks, before shaping the chunks into balls by rolling them between my palms. I press down with the heel of my palm to flatten each ball into a disc, leaving an imprint of my palm lines.

The jiaozi pi shouldn't be perfectly flat. Unlike sheets of pasta rolled out to make ravioli or tortellini, the circle of dough for jiaozi should be thicker in the centre and thinner around the edge. This means the centre can hold the xianr, the filling, without breaking, while the edges can be tightly sealed. I use the edge of a rolling pin to flatten the edge of the circle, rotating it with my other hand. It's the kind of swift movement that I never thought I'd be capable of, but now it comes easily to me, even though I'm hopelessly uncoordinated when it comes to speed and rhythm. When cooking, my body falls into a natural rhythm I didn't know I had.

I take a small spoonful of the chopped filling (peas, tofu, mushrooms, spring onions, garlic and ginger, with a little soy sauce and oyster sauce and sesame oil). I place it in the centre of the circle, then seal it with two or three folds on each side so that the curved outer edge is moulded round my fingers. Every homemade jiaozi looks like this: formed inside a cupped hand, pressed shut by firm fingers. Each dumpling holds the shape of my skin.

◄◄

It's summer in Wellington, and I go swimming with my friend Rose in Oriental Bay in the evening after work. The moon has already risen by late afternoon, a shy arc just visible against deepening blue. We wriggle into our swimsuits beneath the sun and the moon.

Rose, who was born in Shanghai but grew up in Whanganui, swims out to the floating platform and back again three times. I dip my body three-quarters into the water and paddle gently, wary of jellyfish and the stinging cold. We dry off clumsily, becoming aware of the gnawing feeling in our stomachs and a weakening in the backs of our knees. I love swimming, partly because of that particular kind of post-swim hunger that can only compared to hunger after sex. The ache that tells you if you don't go eat something soon your limbs might liquefy. It must have something to do with the weight of water on our muscles, the strain of using parts of our body we never use on land.

With sand still between our toes and thighs, we sit by the window in a Chinese takeaway. We eat bowls of dumplings and noodles and chat over clouds of steam. A Taste of Home – undeniably the best name for a noodle shop – is the only place we've found in Wellington that has thick, chewy hand-pulled noodles and handmade dumplings. We sip peach juice between mouthfuls of soup and chilli oil, cheeks red and eyes watering. I balance a steaming dumpling between my chopsticks while the sea wind beats against the windows.

Acknowledgements

Thanks to Holly Hunter, the editor of *Mimicry*, where "Hungry Girls" was first published in 2016. Other excerpts also appeared in *Food Memory Bank* (foodmemorybank. wordpress.com), created by Rebecca May Johnson, and in *gal-dem*.

Thank you to everyone who read and shared my Shanghai blog posts, which is where this project was born, and to all the friends and family who have folded and eaten dumplings with me.

Lastly, thank you to editors Yen-Yen Lu and Emma Dai'an Wright, who took a chance on this small book and gave it a beautiful, bright home.

About the author

Nina Mingya Powles is a poet, writer and editor from Aotearoa New Zealand. She is the author of *Magnolia* 木蘭 (Nine Arches Press, 2020), which was shortlisted for both the Ondaatje Prize and the Forward Prize for Best First Collection.

In 2018 she won the Women Poets' Prize, awarded by the Rebecca Swift Foundation. In 2019 she won the inaugural Nan Shepherd Prize for her debut collection of essays *Small Bodies of Water*, published by Canongate in 2021. She is the founding editor of Bitter Melon.

Nina was born in Aotearoa, partly grew up in China, and now lives in London.

@ninamingya

About the illustrator

Emma Dai'an Wright is a British-Chinese-Vietnamese publisher and illustrator based between Birmingham and Riga, via Bracknell and Winnersh. She set up The Emma Press in 2012 with the support of the Prince's Trust.

About The Emma Press

The Emma Press is an independent publishing house based in Birmingham, UK. It was founded in 2012 and specialises in poetry, short fiction, and children's books. The Emma Press is passionate about publishing literature which is welcoming and accessible. Find out more about our books here: theemmapress.com

Glossary

Page no.	Romanised term (Cantonese)	Romanised term (Mandarin)	Chinese characters
1		Popo	婆婆
2	Gung Gung		公公
3	yum cha	yincha	饮茶
	charsiubao	chashaobao	叉烧包
4		jiaozi	饺子
		cong youbing	葱油饼
8		Mei guanxi	没关系。
		Wo e si le	我饿死　了。
9		shengjianbao	生煎包
		guotie	锅贴
10		liuxuesheng	留学生
		shaomai	烧卖
		xiaolongbao	小笼包
		shuijiao	水饺
12		xianr	馅儿
14		congyou banmian	葱油拌面
17		meiyu	梅雨
18		cong	葱
		lü	绿
20		boluobao	菠萝包
21	cha chaan teng	chacanting	茶餐厅
22		xiangjiaochuan	香蕉船
23		niunai	牛奶

Page no.	Romanised term (Cantonese)	Romanised term (Mandarin)	Chinese characters
		mianbao	面包
	hargow	xiajiao	虾饺
	siumai	shaomai	烧卖
		luobogao	萝卜糕
24		Ni chi le ma?	你吃了吗？
		Chibao le ma?	吃饱了吗？
34		baozi	包子
		lamian	拉面
35		bing	饼
36		jidanbing	鸡蛋饼
		zhimabing	芝麻饼
		lazhimabing	辣芝麻饼
37		congyoubing	葱油饼
41		zongzi	粽子
42		niangao	年糕
		tangyuan	汤圆
44	lo mai gai	nuomiji	糯米鸡
	dim sum	dianxin	点心
45		mifan	米饭
49	wonton	huntun/yuntun/cha-oshou	馄饨/云吞/抄手
50		hongshaorou	红烧肉
		shizitou	狮子头
51		xiaolongxia	小龙虾
		da huntun	大馄饨

Page no.	Romanised term (Cantonese)	Romanised term (Mandarin)	Chinese characters
		xiao huntun	小馄饨
53	gai lan	jielan	芥兰
55		pu'er	普洱
		youzi	柚子
		shizi	柿子
		qingmei	青梅
56		doufu hua	豆腐花
		jianbing	煎饼
		Yao la ma?	要辣吗？
57		xiaochi	小吃
		biangbiang	See note below
59		xian	燹
60	jyutbeng	yuebing	月饼
62	bokchoi	baicai	白菜
64		qiezi	茄子
69	hofun	hefen	河粉
73		mapo doufu	麻婆豆腐
		niuroumian	牛肉面
75		jiaozi	饺子
76		jiao'er	娇耳
77		Zheli chi, xiexie.	这里吃，谢谢。
83		jiaozi pi	饺子皮

The biangbiang character is very complicated! More information on the character may be found at https://en.wikipedia.org/wiki/Biangbiang_noodles